T0365781

EMOTRY
SELF EXPRESSION

Janelle James

AuthorHouse™
1663 Liberty Drive
Bloomington, IN 47403
www.authorhouse.com
Phone: 1-800-839-8640

© 2014, 2015 Janelle James. All rights reserved.

No part of this book may be reproduced, stored in a retrieval system, or transmitted by any means without the written permission of the author.

Published by AuthorHouse 12/29/2014

ISBN: 978-1-4969-5019-2 (sc)
ISBN: 978-1-4969-5020-8 (e)

Library of Congress Control Number: 2014919768

Any people depicted in stock imagery provided by Thinkstock are models, and such images are being used for illustrative purposes only. Certain stock imagery © Thinkstock.

This book is printed on acid-free paper.

Because of the dynamic nature of the Internet, any web addresses or links contained in this book may have changed since publication and may no longer be valid. The views expressed in this work are solely those of the author and do not necessarily reflect the views of the publisher, and the publisher hereby disclaims any responsibility for them.

authorHOUSE®

For Lionel James
Father, Advisor, Guardian Angel

If it was NOT for him I would of
NEVER
put pen to paper
thoughts to black and white

R.I.P Dad

Ackowledgements

God wrote my path long before I was born and in my story I had to experience different trials and tribulations to reach various achievements in my life but I could not do it on my own so he made sure my path crossed with different people and whether they didn't stay long like aquientences or if they stuck by my side through ALL my pitfalls as friends. Those few friends became family and with my family they pushed me, forced me to chanllenge the norm & my doubts and face my fears.

This strength that they gave me forced me to step out of my comfort zone and write and publish this book.

Ones voice is a very important and useful instrument.

If properly used it can be used to power dreams, promote people, express ones emotions BUT on the other side it is THE most deadliest weapon a human being can possess.

Society will use the words "self expression" as a negative word to describe someones unique way of dressing their skin such as clothing, piercing and hair colour just to name a few. What one must understand is that there is NO normality to ones self expressions this is why we must NOT judge what we do not understand.

When we find our voice we can best express our emotions as well as give people a better understanding as to who we REALLY are.

Expression is the way one finds out who they really are through writing or any form of creativity.

Visual art such as painting and drawing were my first forms of self-expression. Then I picked up a camera and my eyes were seeing things no one saw or took the time to see. My dad used to tell me to capture and appreciate ALL that God has blessed me with for there is beauty in EVERYTHING.

Then my Dad died and I got lost until I picked up a pen and started to write. Feelings and emotions that I didn't know I had just started to pour out of me. My buried dreams and tucked away thoughts were in front of me in black and white and I did not know what to do BUT continue to write.

Writing became an outcome for me to learn about myself and the more I wrote the more I began to realise who I was.

WHO IS SHE??

I look at the pictures
I wonder who is she?
My name is the subject of the album
I am tagged in the picture
BUT seriously
WHO IS SHE?

I look into her eyes
what stares back
is something strange
you are told that the eyes
are windows to ones SOUL
BUT her's is lost
SHE does not know
WHO SHE IS?

She seems to be trapped
She is yearning to get out
She wants to be the person she used to be
But she is afraid
Not sure what she is afraid of

She used to be a free spirit
Now EVERYTHING scares her
But what scares her the most
is trying to figure out

WHO SHE IS?

She is a Daughter; a Sister; an Aunt
She is a Niece; a Cousin
She is a Friend; a Woman

BUT WHAT DEFINES HER?

WHO IS SHE?????

JOURNEY PREPARATIONS

When one prepares to go on a trip
a destination must be decided
my destination is
SELF

What do I pack?
Do I travel light or heavy?
As I look around my room & my closet
Do I pack my comfy clothes or the clothes
that show the REAL ME

Am I ready........?
Who is the REAL ME
I ask myself EVERYDAY
WHO AM I ????

Flawless I am NOT
My Butt sags, my Thighs rub together
I have a formation of a muffin top
and my breast seems to be moving
to MY under arms
so COMFY clothes it is

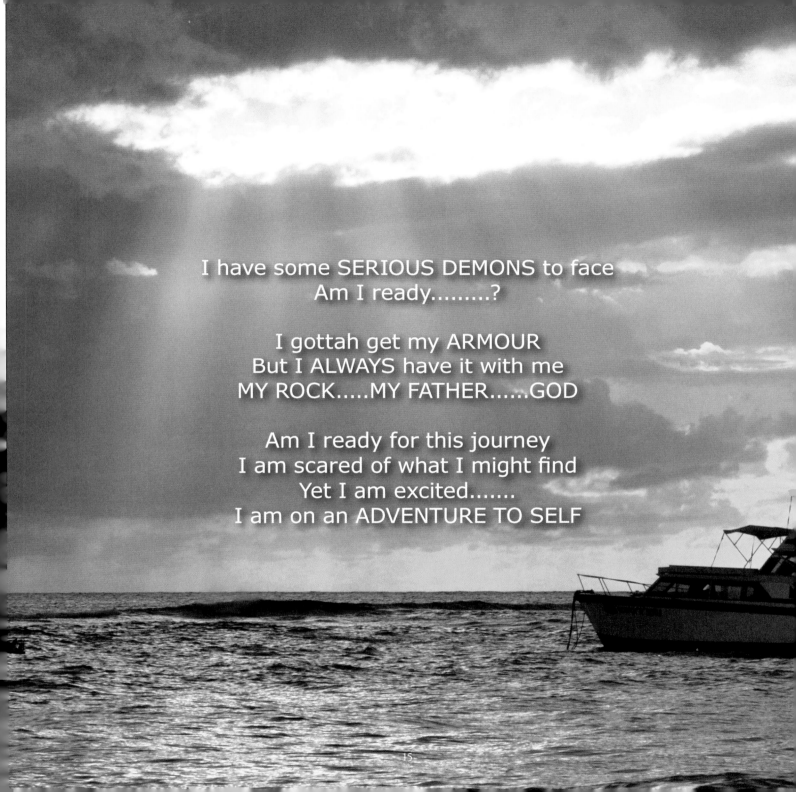

I have some SERIOUS DEMONS to face
Am I ready.........?

I gottah get my ARMOUR
But I ALWAYS have it with me
MY ROCK.....MY FATHER......GOD

Am I ready for this journey
I am scared of what I might find
Yet I am excited.......
I am on an ADVENTURE TO SELF

MISDIRECTION

MISDIRECTION is
What the eyes see and
the ears hear
the mind believes

I smile and I laugh A LOT
MISDIRECTION
"I am FINE"; "I UNDERSTAND"
"No Problem"
MISDIRECTION

MISDIRECTION is easier
than dealing with my Demon
Low SELF-ESTEEM

Truth is I am NOT fine
I have a Demon and
it haunts me
EVERYDAY

MISDIRECTION is my
brick wall which
prevents me from
realizing the TRUTH

TRUTH is
I AM PERFECT
JUST THE WAY
I AM

BROKEN

I don't understand WHY
What did I do to deserve
the PAIN
THE EMBARRASSMENT

All I ever tried to be
was a friend
a SPECIAL FRIEND
MORE THAN a FRIEND

You knew how I felt
cause I told you
I NEVER hid my feelings
from you

You KNEW that I liked
being with you
and you played with my
emotions

Your favorite line was
"I am working / I am gunna come over"
BUT you don't without a warning
and with NO APOLOGY

Yet I forgave you
I'm trusting that way
and you used me
You used ALL my
insecurities against me

26

You told me once
that you could see
a future with me
was that even true

You told me A LOT
Now I don't know
what to believe
was any of it true

And now you tell me
that "you are making AN
EFFORT NOW to see me
and that you weren't REALLY
making a BIG effort before"

You didn't like my company
you never REALLY liked me
We been doing this for
a little over a year

All this time it was a chore
you had to make an EFFORT
to see me
I didn't realize

I don't understand
what changed?
FOUR months
I seen you once in
FOUR MONTHS

Now ALL of a sudden
I am to believe that
YOU MISS ME
when you spoke those words BEFORE

How do you think that makes me feel
Shit I don't even know how
I feel so many emotions
but one stands out
STUPID

I didn't realize that
I was such a chore to be with
that EFFORT has to be put in
that I have to be lied to

What did I do to deserve that?
NO apology NOTHING
NOTHING he says can help
NOTHING can make me feel BETTER

How could someone do that?
Only a SELFISH PERSON
can behave that way
and sleep when the night come

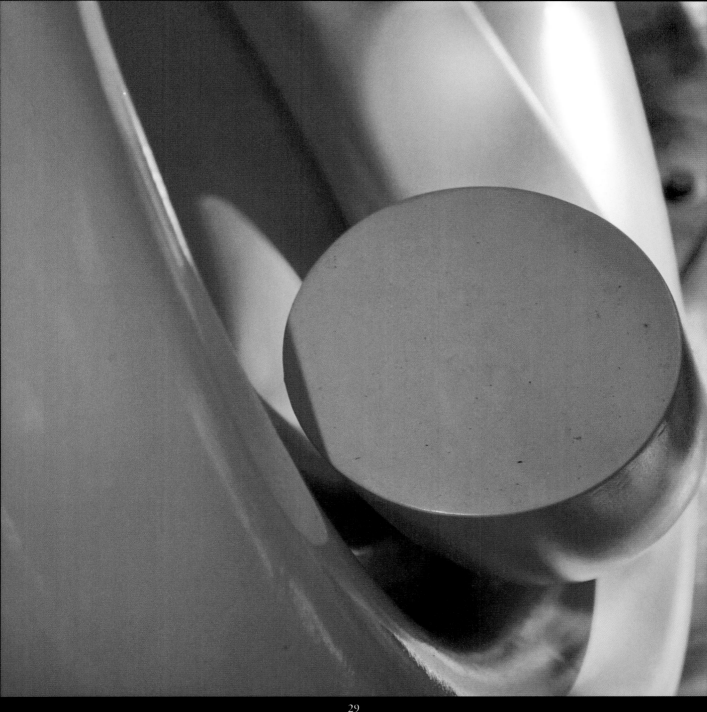

OLE SOUL

It is one of those HOTT Summer nights
so I sit outside looking up at the moon
music is playing in the background
and I hear sweet instrumentals and
then suddenly Ella's voice chimes in
"Summer time and the living is easy
Fish are jumping and the cotton is high"

I lean back on my stairs as I close my eyes
I think of those Sunday afternoons
when my father had TOTAL control of the record player
He would walk in after a good game of tennis
stepping over bodies lying in front the TV
while making a B line for the record player
suddenly you would hear the sweet horn of Chuck Mangione

That was our cue....with out words.....we knew......"TV DUN"

SUDDENLY I have the BAHJESUS scared right out of me
a car rolls up at 5 miles an hour right past my house
it is at this point I think to myself "he musse deaf"
he is blasting what he thinks must be "music"
I hear some of the lyrics "Yuh pum pum clean and ready,
Suh mi dash weh di boots, And mi cum inna yuh belly
Giddy up pon di cocky"

Wha de rass.....? Is this what young people listen too?
I look round to see if ANYONE else heard it
suddenly panic grips my SHAKING body
I begin to think of my nephew and his friends
Impressionable young boys

Is that where they gunna get tips from....REALLY
There was and is NO WAY a man can come up on me wid
psst "my sexy red friend, you want dis"
without me looking at him with a straight face
and asking him if he really thinks that line would get me to say
"OKAY....Baby let's go"
What are you thinking? .... Are you thinking?

A song suddenly comes to mind
"Come on and go with me
Come on over to my place"
Teddy knew how to talk to a woman
Do these guys in our society think that
it would take away from their manhood
If they spoke or treated us women with some respect

What happened to men opening doors.....
Pulling out de chair for woman?
What happened to men who actually wear MEN'S pants
that don't show their underwear?
What happened to men who can romance a woman
instead of jus trying to get into their pants?
What happened to men who actually care what they look like,
smell like before they approach a woman?
WHAT HAPPEN TO MEN?......cause
ALL I see are little boys in a grown man's body

STUPPPPPPEEEEEESSSSSS

As I pull myself together to go inside
I think to myself "I was born in the wrong era"

I jus have an

OLE SOUL

HIP HOP

I remember the first time I saw her
My Brother brought her home

I was 10 yrs old and in AWE of her
she was so BRIGHT and when she spoke
It was pure HONESTY

She soon became a fixture in our house
.......actually as I think back Mummy
Used to get tired of hearing her
To a point we would sometimes
Have to sneak her in

BUT we LOVED her
So when we got caught and our
ASSES cut we bore the pain
Cause we knew she was worth it

I used to see her in fetes and house parties
She was the HOTTEST thing
And everyone wanted to be her

You knew when she was in the room
Cause she had the attention of EVERYONE
Old and young, with her
Attitude, Style and language

Listening and watching her used to
take us to places we could only DREAM OF

When we copied her style of
Fashion and speech we felt as if
We were a part of her

Her life gave us a new meaning to ours

As we got older we noticed a difference in her
She was changing and not for the good
She seemed to have lost her soul
Her sense of worth

and with that her VALUES

She became so overwhelmed with popularity
That she became CHEAP and everyone had her

She no longer educated us about our
HISTORY or taught us SELF WORTH

She was into VIOLENCE, GUNS, GANGS,
MONEY, SEX and DRUGS

Her loyal followers tried to keep her
On the straight and narrow but it
Was the BLING and the FLASHING
Lights that had her attention

It became TOO much for her

We realised that she was
Getting lost in the crowd

But we would see her sometimes
but only briefly and
With someone from her past

People say she died with the new generation
But this is the Generation who NEEDS her

I believe she has just lost her way

Help me find her
I LOVE HER
And MISS HER
She is

HIP HOP

PISSED OFF

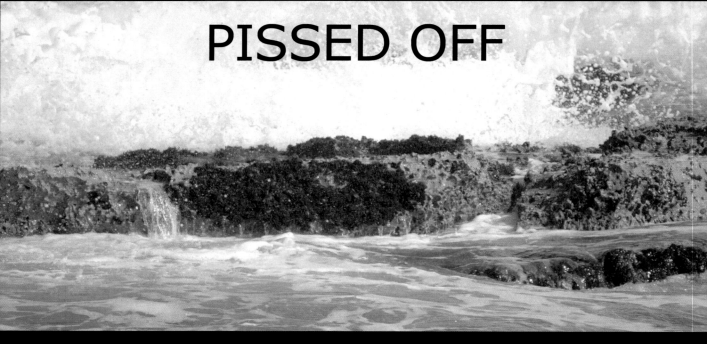

She grew accustom
To the special treatment
Which he showed her

The singing
The compliments
The way his face lite up
When he saw her on FaceTime
The sound of his voice on the phone

She loved the way
He made her feel
She never felt this way

But today was
Different
There was no

Special greeting
No compliments on the pics
No I miss you
No I love you

I got worried
Scared even
Then
I got pissed off
Mad as hell even

All I wanted was
"Hi can't message right now"
"not alone" ANYTHING

Anything DAMN IT

YOU

You told me to find
someone else
someone other than

YOU

Someone who is ready for love
Someone ready like me

BUT...

There is no one else
Relationship after relationship
Heartache after heartache
I ALWAYS returned to

YOU

You are HOME
I return to YOU
To find the ME

The me
I lost

I return to YOU
Because you remind me
Of who I was

Of who I AM

I return to YOU

Because

I LOVE who I am
When I am with YOU

I don't have to hide
ME from

YOU

YOU MAKE ME SICK

I AM PISSED

You make me SICK

You stand there
Smiling
Looking like
You look

YOU MAKE ME SICK

You are either
Clueless or
Smart as
SHITE

YOU MAKE ME SICK

IT PISSES
ME OFF......

That you can't see
The effect you have
On ME

Just the thought
Of SEEING YOU

Hearing your voice
Receiving a call
Message
From you

Sends my
Mental and physical
Chemicals
Under a 'Spell'

My heart beats
A little faster

My palms get
Sweaty

My hands
Start to shake

Then my body

Well like I said
Under a spell

Baby you
LITERALLY

MAKE ME SICK

SILENCE

When I speak
Do you
Listen

Do you listen
To my words
Or my
Silence

My unspoken words
Of pain
Suffering
Hunger for

LOVE

My silence
Speaks of
Suicide
Death

My death
My pain
My suffering

Years of silence
Goes unheard
But can you
Handle my silence

Are you willing
To listen and
Understand
MY
SILENCE

Sometimes I
Can't understand it
For I am surrounded
By people who
Say they
Love me

Yet I felt nothing but
Loneliness
Because
NO ONE
Listened to
MY SILENCE

YEARS AND YEARS

Years and years
Of putting feelings
under the carpet

Years and years
Of being strong
Of NOT showing

PAIN

Years and years
Of keeping my
Feelings

HIDDEN

Years and years
Of smiling
And laughing
Through the

PAIN

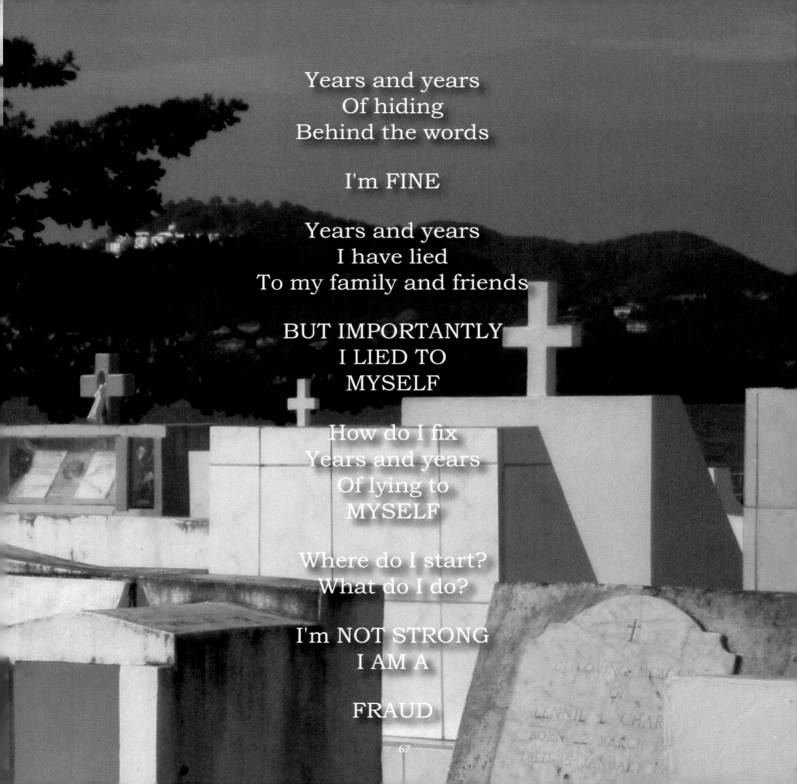

Years and years
Of hiding
Behind the words

I'm FINE

Years and years
I have lied
To my family and friends

BUT IMPORTANTLY
I LIED TO
MYSELF

How do I fix
Years and years
Of lying to
MYSELF

Where do I start?
What do I do?

I'm NOT STRONG
I AM A

FRAUD

Janelle James is an artist in
EVERY sense of the word from her
photography to her writing shows
sensitivity and imagination.

Janelle taught herself photography
by using her camera as her eyes.
With EVERY shot she became one
with the subject and with that she
captures their soul.

As a writer she put her heart and
soul on paper. She held nothing
back because she believed in being
honest..100% honesty. She felt
that if she was honest it would let
her readers know that they
were / are NOT alone.

Printed in the United States
By Bookmasters